Seasons
of the
Witch
SAMHAIN JOURNAL

Lorriane Anderson

ROCKPOOL

"It is not the answer
that enlightens,
but the question."

– Eugène Ionesco

Welcome, Sacred Soul ...

This journal is an expansion of the themes found within the *Seasons of the Witch: Samhain Oracle*. Though these themes are most apparent at Samhain, you may find them popping up at other times of the year, too, and certainly throughout your life.

So many are chasing the answers to the wrong questions. The right question will unlock your soul, allowing the beauty of what is already within you to appear. Within these pages, you will find 50 journal prompts to help you to find the right answers to the right questions. But this is your space. Use this journal in the way that aligns most with your soul. Feel free to jump straight to a page you are called to, or intuitively select a page the way you would pull an oracle card. Allow your soul to guide you to what you need most.

You will find plenty of free journaling pages here to allow your spirit the space to expand. Some of these pages are lined while others have been left unlined so you can let your creativity unfurl. Explore your freedom here, knowing these pages are here to hold your secrets, protect your fears, and share in your success.

All Hallows' Eve

Do not be afraid of your inner power, sacred one. Call it
forth. Imagine what it would feel like if you did not limit
the raw force within you. Describe this feeling here.

_____

_____

_____

_____

_____

_____

_____

_____

_____

_____

_____

_____

_____

_____

_____

_____

Altar

What's most important to you? What things represent joyous
memories, loved ones, or the passions within your soul? Journal about
them here. Why do they bring you joy or profound connection?
And if you are called to do so, build an altar with these objects
to lift your joy off the page and infuse it into the everyday.

Ancestors

Write a letter to an ancestor. There is no need to know their name, their face, or their story, for their connection to you flows through your veins. Give them your hardships or share with them your joys. Allow this connection to form upon these sacred pages.

Apples

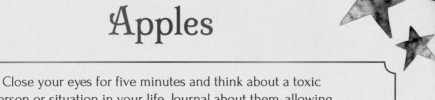

Close your eyes for five minutes and think about a toxic
person or situation in your life. Journal about them, allowing
yourself to see see their poison for what it truly is.

_____

_____

_____

_____

_____

_____

_____

_____

_____

_____

_____

_____

_____

_____

_____

_____

_____

Banshee

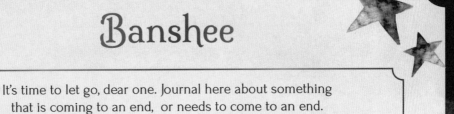

It's time to let go, dear one. Journal here about something
that is coming to an end, or needs to come to an end.

_____

_____

_____

_____

_____

_____

_____

_____

_____

_____

_____

_____

_____

_____

Bat

Use this space to log your intuitive downloads. Write down anything that feels significant. Colors, shapes, animals, feelings ... if it feels important, that's because it is.

Black Cat

Where do you need to establish more boundaries?

_____

_____

_____

_____

_____

_____

_____

_____

_____

_____

_____

_____

_____

_____

_____

_____

_____

Broom

Make a list of everything you'd like to do, have, or call into existence. Now reduce this list by half. The remaining list is what your soul needs most.

_____

_____

_____

_____

_____

_____

_____

_____

_____

_____

_____

_____

Candle Magic

Write a letter to the universe by candlelight,
describing your deepest desires.

_____

_____

_____

_____

_____

_____

_____

_____

_____

_____

_____

_____

_____

_____

_____

_____

_____

_____

Cauldron

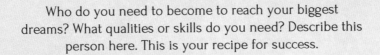

Who do you need to become to reach your biggest
dreams? What qualities or skills do you need? Describe this
person here. This is your recipe for success.

_____

_____

_____

_____

_____

_____

_____

_____

_____

_____

_____

_____

_____

_____

_____

_____

_____

Centaur

Make a list of your needs, then review it with honesty and sincerity. How much of your list are truly needs? How much is lustful temptation? Find clarity within these pages.

_____

_____

_____

_____

_____

_____

_____

_____

_____

_____

_____

_____

_____

_____

_____

_____

_____

Chalice

How well do you know your body? How often are you mindful
of the feelings of the heart? Take some time to journal
about the relationship you have with yourself and how you
can offer yourself more support and nourishment.

_____

_____

_____

_____

_____

_____

_____

_____

_____

_____

_____

_____

Coming of Winter

Reflect upon the past year without judgment.
Acknowledge your successes and learn from your failures.

_____

_____

_____

_____

_____

_____

_____

_____

_____

_____

_____

_____

_____

_____

Coven

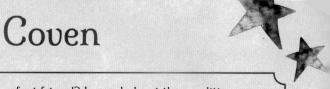

What is your idea of a perfect friend? Journal about the qualities they would have, what kind of things they would do, and how they would support you as a friend. Do you have a friend like this in your life? If not, now you know what to look for.

_____

_____

_____

_____

_____

_____

_____

_____

_____

_____

_____

_____

_____

_____

_____

_____

Crystals and Herbs

Spend time in nature, then return to these pages and
journal about your time with Mother Earth.

_____

_____

_____

_____

_____

_____

_____

_____

_____

_____

_____

_____

_____

_____

_____

_____

Dark Moon

What are your biggest dreams right now? Do you need to
think bigger? Do you need to think smaller? Explain.

_____

_____

_____

_____

_____

_____

_____

_____

_____

_____

_____

_____

_____

_____

_____

_____

Divination

Shuffle the cards of any oracle or tarot deck until one falls from the stack. Meditate upon the image on the card, then write about the guidance you've intuitively received. Do not read from the guidebook. Trust yourself to know the answer.

_____

_____

_____

_____

_____

_____

_____

_____

_____

_____

_____

_____

_____

_____

_____

_____

_____

_____

Elders

Think of an Elder in your family or a mentor from your life. Describe the advice they'd give you. How can you apply this advice to your life today?

_____

_____

_____

_____

_____

_____

_____

_____

_____

_____

_____

_____

_____

Elements

How do you feel today? In meditation, ask your emotions to show you what they need you to know and journal about it here.

Frog

What's changing or shifting in your life right now?
How will this transform your life for the better?

_____

_____

_____

_____

_____

_____

_____

_____

_____

_____

_____

_____

_____

_____

_____

_____

Ghost

Is there a situation you have played over in your head again and again? Journal about it here. Why does it still haunt you? What would you do differently? What do you believe you need in order to move on?

_____

_____

_____

_____

_____

_____

_____

_____

_____

_____

_____

_____

_____

_____

_____

_____

Graveyard

Journal about everything that is within your control. These
are the things that will bring you peace. Focus on them
instead of focusing on what you can't control.

_____

_____

_____

_____

_____

_____

_____

_____

_____

_____

_____

_____

_____

_____

_____

_____

_____

_____

Greet the Darkness

Confront your fears here upon these sacred pages.

_____

_____

_____

_____

_____

_____

_____

_____

_____

_____

_____

_____

_____

_____

_____

_____

_____

_____

Grief

Write about lost dreams, hopes, or loved ones. Allow yourself
this time to mourn these losses upon these sacred pages.

_____

_____

_____

_____

_____

_____

_____

_____

_____

_____

_____

_____

_____

_____

_____

_____

Haunted

To whom do you owe an apology? Write a letter to them upon this page. You can also apologize to yourself if you feel the need to do so.

_____

_____

_____

_____

_____

_____

_____

_____

_____

_____

_____

_____

_____

_____

_____

Healer

_____

_____

_____

_____

_____

_____

_____

_____

_____

_____

_____

_____

_____

_____

Intuition

How can your ego and higher self work together for your highest good?

Journey

Describe your life from your earliest memory until now.
Allow this journey to show you the perfection of the path
you have walked and the clues to where you are going.

_____

_____

_____

_____

_____

_____

_____

_____

_____

_____

_____

_____

_____

_____

_____

_____

Mischief

Have some fun upon this page. Draw, color – wreck this page!

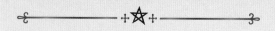

Nature Spirits

Journal about the small but important things in life that have missed out on your attention lately. Call them forth and be reminded of their significance.

_____

_____

_____

_____

_____

_____

_____

_____

_____

_____

_____

_____

_____

_____

_____

_____

_____

_____

Owl

Spend time outside at night. Close your eyes, listen to the sounds of the night, and journal about this experience here.

Potions and Spells

Try your hand at writing a spell, potion, or recipe upon these pages.
Then work the spell and journal about its effectiveness.

_____

_____

_____

_____

_____

_____

_____

_____

_____

_____

_____

_____

_____

_____

_____

_____

Protection

Leave your worries here upon these sacred pages.
As you write, know your fears are kept secret within this
journal where no one can use them against you.

_____

_____

_____

_____

_____

_____

_____

_____

_____

_____

_____

_____

_____

_____

_____

_____

Pumpkin

Who makes you feel protected and supported? Why?

_____

_____

_____

_____

_____

_____

_____

_____

_____

_____

_____

_____

_____

_____

_____

_____

_____

_____

_____

_____

_____

Raven

A message is waiting for you. Ask a question out loud, then begin to journal without stopping. Don't read your entry until you have completely finished. You will find the answer within what you have written.

Rebirth

What would happen if you started over again, knowing what
you know now? How would your life be different?

_____

_____

_____

_____

_____

_____

_____

_____

_____

_____

_____

_____

_____

_____

_____

_____

_____

_____

_____

_____

_____

Reflection

Upon these sacred pages, face the false statements you've told
yourself. Reflect upon how negative self-talk is holding you back.

_____

_____

_____

_____

_____

_____

_____

_____

_____

_____

_____

_____

_____

_____

_____

_____

Ritual

Create a self-care ritual here. Put this ritual into action,
then return to these pages to journal about the experience.

Rooted

Don't give up, sacred one. Write, draw, or wreck this page.
Brainstorm here and allow your magic to unfurl.

Seduction

What are your temptations? What do they
offer you? What do they cost you?

_____

_____

_____

_____

_____

_____

_____

_____

_____

_____

_____

_____

_____

_____

_____

_____

_____

Silence

Sit in silence for no less than 10 minutes. How did it feel to be still?

_____

_____

_____

_____

_____

_____

_____

_____

_____

_____

_____

_____

_____

_____

_____

_____

Skull

What would you want your obituary to say?
Are you doing these things, and if not, why?

Spider

Do you believe you are capable of incredible manifestations?
How have you doubted your magic?

_____

_____

_____

_____

_____

_____

_____

_____

_____

_____

_____

_____

_____

_____

_____

_____

Third Harvest

Celebrate your accomplishments upon these sacred pages.
Do not hold back: you're awesome, so own it!

Transformation

What are some resources you have not allowed yourself
to explore? How can you make use of them now?

_____

_____

_____

_____

_____

_____

_____

_____

_____

_____

_____

_____

_____

_____

_____

The Underworld

Are you jealous of or angry at someone? Journal about these feelings
here, then send that person the energy of love and well wishes.

The Veil

Journal about the first person who comes to mind. What is your soul trying to tell you about them?

_____

_____

_____

_____

_____

_____

_____

_____

_____

_____

_____

_____

_____

_____

Voices

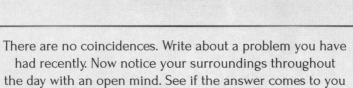

There are no coincidences. Write about a problem you have had recently. Now notice your surroundings throughout the day with an open mind. See if the answer comes to you and return to this page to record the experience.

_____

_____

_____

_____

_____

_____

_____

_____

_____

_____

_____

_____

Witch

What does the word "witch" mean to you? Free your mind of social conditioning and allow the truth of this word to present itself to you.

_____

_____

_____

_____

_____

_____

_____

_____

_____

_____

_____

_____

_____

_____

_____

_____

_____

Wolf

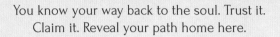

You know your way back to the soul. Trust it.
Claim it. Reveal your path home here.

_____

_____

_____

_____

_____

_____

_____

_____

_____

_____

_____

_____

_____

_____

_____

_____